Getting Started with Project Management

Getting Started with Project Management

Managing Projects in Small Bites

Chiji A. Ohayia, Ph.D., PMP

GETTING STARTED WITH PROJECT MANAGEMENT
MANAGING PROJECTS IN SMALL BITES

iUniverse books may be ordered through booksellers or by contacting:

iUniverse
1663 Liberty Drive
Bloomington, IN 47403
www.iuniverse.com
1-800-Authors (1-800-288-4677)

ISBN: 978-1-5320-0741-5 (sc)
ISBN: 978-1-5320-0742-2 (e)

Library of Congress Control Number: 2016915756

Print information available on the last page.

iUniverse rev. date: 10/05/2016

To my family and friends for their unwavering support.

To project management students and practitioners who bring efficiency to organizations.

To the spirit and memories of my parents, whom I affectionately refer to as Joe-Helen.

Contents

Preview

Managing Projects in Small Bites (MPSB) is a series of handbooks designed to introduce various project management concepts in a uniquely focused bite size. Fundamentally, project management is the planning and arrangement of an organization's resources in order to effectively and efficiently move a specific task, event, or duty to completion. Through framework and tactics, this practical approach can be readily applied to facilitate a project's delivery.

Two of the most popular project management (PM) approaches are the *Project Management Body of Knowledge* (PMBOK) guide and *PRojects IN Controlled Environments* (PRINCE2). PMBOK is used as the foundation to each handbook in the series, providing a simplified, comprehensible explanation of project-management principles.

- The guide's predecessors, which include long-form texts in the field of PM, have engaged and both formally and informally trained thousands of practitioners over the last fifty years. Personally, these books have served as the foundation for my extensive experience in project management—as a student, researcher, practitioner, consultant, and instructor. I am greatly indebted to their accomplishments, particularly the PMBOK approach.

- A common misconception about PM is that it is an overly daunting profession. This has been sustained by the sheer size of textbooks that are available to a prospective practitioner—for example, the fifth-edition PMBOK is nearly six hundred pages!
- Much like the legacy guides, the advent of the Internet has afforded many new project managers the opportunity to explore and search topics of interest at great depth while also allowing them to gain a tacit understanding of broad subject matters.
- By providing a quick project-management framework—complete with background information and sample scenarios—MPSB enables the practitioner to gain the requisite initial exposure (or refresher) and readily implement procedures to boost his or her daily productivity.

This handbook is useful for anyone interested in the discipline of project management, from the casually curious to seasoned practitioner. Each handbook in the series provides a simplified explanation of a particular project-management concept. When you are on the go, MPSB will ground your knowledge with a clear and formalized guide that can be used to organize any project.

Introduction

I began my career in the mid-1980s with the New York City Department of Sanitation as an Assistant Project Coordinator supporting the Telecommunications Department. My first assignment was to assist with the upgrade of all the telephone systems in the sanitation garages throughout the five boroughs of New York City (the Bronx, Brooklyn, Manhattan, Queens, and Staten Island). This was at a period when the field of project management as we know it today was relative in its infancy. To put this is a proper context: the Project Management Institute (PMI) published the first PMBOK guide in 1996 with 179 pages. The current PMBOK, the fifth edition, has 589 pages. Needless to say, in the mid-1980s and early 1990s, my colleagues and I had limited access to resources.

Although the field of project management has undergone substantial evolution over the last one hundred years, its description has remained relatively static. *Project management* has become a household term in many industries: aerospace, construction, health care, and information technology, to name a few. This focus has allowed these organizations to employ some aspect of project management to guide the delivery of project objectives.

The discipline helps organizations become more efficient in utilizing resources. Competition and customer expectations have made project-management principles the dominant methods for success by providing a common understanding of steps and roles that can apply to a project.

As both an art and science, the project-management processes offered in the MPSB handbooks illustrate the science, such as systematic approaches that use a standard process, while the art is portrayed through various scenarios and examples.

Purpose of a Specific Book in the Context of the Series

A restorative project manager instinctively knows when and how to resolve project issues. Getting started with project management is the first step toward building requisite skills to be a successful project manager. In this first volume of the series, the reader is introduced to a cooking event in order to show the project selection process. By the end of this book, the reader should gain a better understanding of project-management concepts and the essential skills required to manage projects.

The first two, "What is a Project?" and "What is Project Management?" provide an extended definition through a quick review of the field's evolution. The third section, "Project Management Framework," arranges the interdisciplinary factors of the field. Intertwined within these sections is a cooking scenario that serves as a practical example for discussing various project management concepts. Section 5 describes the role of a project manager and the key function in the project management process.

Key Lessons

This handbook is intended to introduce project management concepts in a consumable format. It serves as a valuable quick reference for experienced project managers as well as a guide new or part-time managers to build a solid foundation with project management concepts. Henceforth, the breakdown of the text will consist of the following:

- PM terms, framework, and scenarios
- Underlying PM principles
- HOW: the application
- Intermittent tips and references for further reading

> *Other terms for project management include methods, techniques, practices, methodologies, processes, frameworks, or tools; some use all these (and other) terms interchangeably.*

In this section, an elaborative definition of a project is provided. A project should be defined by asking some basic key questions:

- What is the activity to be taken, and what are the end results (the prize)?
- How much will a project like this cost?
- Are we capable of doing this project?
- What is the duration of the project?

> Project - A temporary endeavor undertaken to create a unique product or service. A project has a specific begin date and end date, specific objectives and specific resources assigned to perform the work.

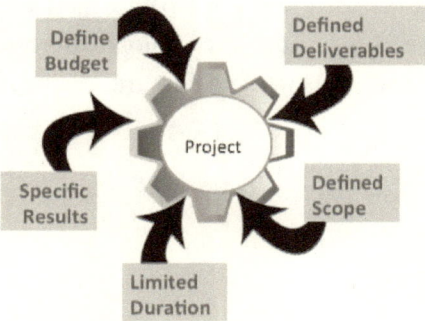

Several definitions exist for the word *project*. James Lewis sees *project* as "a 'problem,' or gap between where something is and where it needs to be, confronted by obstacles that prevent easy movement to close the gap."

Regardless of which definition you choose, every project you manage will have many of the same characteristics. I have adopted the PMBOK (fifth edition) definition of a project: "a temporary endeavor undertaken to create a unique product, service, or result" (pg. 3). The necessary constraints of time, objectives, and resources work on a progressively elaborated output through budgeting, deliverables, and scope creation.

> *"Progressively elaborated" means the characteristics of the product or service of the project are determined incrementally and continually refined and worked out in detail as the project progresses (or requirements unfold).*

The Difference between Projects and Nonprojects

The terms *projects* and *process activities* are often used interchangeably because of incomplete understandings of the differences. While there are significant similarities between project and nonproject activities—for example, both are planned, executed, and controlled activities performed by people under constrained resources—there are major differences. The chart below provides a comparison of project and nonproject operations.

Activity	Objectives	Time	Budget
Project	Projects are undertaken to produce a certain output. If it is a construction-related project, it may produce any tangible structure.	Definitive start and end dates.	Projects are given a fixed budget.
Non-Project / Operations	Operations don't produce anything new, but they are necessary to maintain and sustain the system.	Ongoing activity with no definitive end date.	Operations have to earn profits in order to run the business.

Examples			
Activity	**Project**	**Non Project / Operations**	**Explanation**
Mowing a Lawn		X	This activity is repeated at least several times during the summer months.
Installing a pool in your	X		This is a unique activity, usually a onetime effort, has a definite start and end date, and may be progressively elaborated
Writing a book	X		Predominantly a one-time endeavor
Writing blog posts		X	Usually a repeated tasks – unless you are developing an exclusive piece

Projects are complex, requiring the coordinated undertaking of interrelated activities. Often referred to as a system, a whole made up of connected parts, the complexity of a project requires a consistent, proven methodology to understand and deliver service within an approved budget, scope, and schedule.

Nonproject work or operations work is continuous and repetitious. Furthermore, operational activity does not have an end date. Ongoing activities, such as supervising a work team, running a production process, or operating a manufacturing facility, are not projects. In a nutshell, projects are undertaken to accomplish three things: generate profit, improve process, and/or resolve problems.

What do the Freedom Tower, Facebook's web page design, the Academy Awards, a presidential campaign, and the last meal you ordered (or cooked) all have in common? They're all projects!

Project come in all sizes

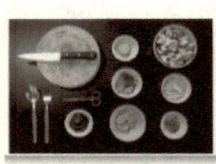  

Small Projects (Cooking)
- Simple Organization
- Few Individuals
- Two or three activities

Medium Projects (Playground)
- Simple Organization
- Many Individuals
- Many activities

Large Projects (Bridges)
- Complex Organization
- Individuals organized as teams
- Divided into stages and/or phases

Projects come in different sizes, ranging from weekend projects, such as painting a room or cleaning gutters, to mega structure projects, like highway construction. In theory, projects can last for one hour, one hundred hours, or hundreds of hours, as they have a consistent presence in our lives.

Reason and Application

> *One must recognize that although the creation of a small deliverable is a project, it should not require the structure and rigor of a much larger project. Complex projects may cross several organizations internal and external to a company. The level of project complexity will determine the expertise needed from project managers, end-to-end directors, and program managers.*

Hunger is a problem that people experience every day; one might even argue that our appetites are the foundation of the economy. Although it is crucial to one's appetite, hunger can be a vital obstacle against productivity if it goes unresolved. Though the stakes may vary, the core argument remains. To illustrate, I will use the idea of cooking a meal for twenty guests as a project.

Imagine that you are planning a big brunch for twenty guests in celebration of a major life event. Known as the foodie among your peers, you and a friend were nominated to host brunch—to which you gladly obliged, as this is an opportunity to show off your skills. You and your friend, whose pairing we will refer to as C&J for the remainder of the text, were commissioned on short notice (one week) to prepare the meal. Fortunately, a friend recently recommended a framework that you plan to use to keep track of tasks and help you meet your deadline.

> **The C&J brunch will be used to illustrate the various project management concepts through discussion of the principles (the science) and the application (the art). This will make the topics come alive in each series of the handbook.**

Requirements/Objectives

Every project starts with a requirement—the purpose that describes the need, justifies why the project is needed, and offers a conjecture on the output's value. Describe the results to be considered throughout the project by asking the following questions. See illustration detailed in the figure below.

- What value should this project produce?
- What constraints will the team face?
- What requirements must be met?
- How will the objectives be satisfied?
- What quality measures and standards must be met?

Answers to these questions will aid in establishing the scope of work. "The work that needs to be accomplished to deliver the results of the project with specified features and functions" (Ganesh 2012, 16).

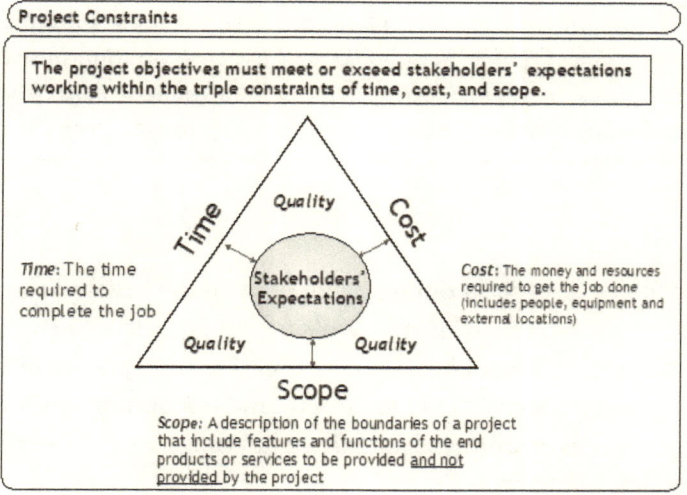

The requirements of the C&J brunch is to

- cook a brunch for twenty guests,
- create a menu to satisfy hunger for twenty guests,
- determine a budget,
- provide a guest list and invitations.
- serve dinner on the third Saturday of June,
- complete the project by June 30

The Scope

This is a high-level description of the possible solutions to the requirement—essentially, the work that needs to be done to deliver the results of the project with specified features and functions (Ganesh 2013).

> *This handbook will address how the C&J brunch was initiated as a project. Other handbooks will use consumption-based activities to explore other project management concepts, including planning, execution, and closing out the project.*

Specific Comparison

The science or process of managing projects comes alive through application of the various project management principles. Specifically, this sample project illustrates the various project-management concepts covered in this and upcoming handbooks. The project is introduced in this handbook to help the reader understand how projects are initiated.

So how should you start? Well, according to Dr. Stephen Covey, the author *The Seven Habits of Highly Effective People*, you should "begin with the end in mind." The end is the prize or value you will receive at the end of the project.

The goal is to serve a delicious meal for the guests on the date as planned, within the specified and agreed upon budget, and exceed guests' (customers') expectations (requirements).

The success of any project hinges on customer acceptance. If the customer rejects the product, the project will be deemed as a failure. To avoid this situation, it is important to have a clear understanding of the project scope and deliverables. Asking open-ended questions during the client/customer interview will help to confirm requirement.

> **The success of any assortment of projects often hinges on the performance level of initiation in a primary project. Without a sound framework, most projects will falter—or even worse, not begin.**

Key Lessons

- developed understanding of project's multifaceted processes
- clarified personal experiences wherein you have already acted as a project manager
- introduced the difference between project and process
- identified that projects are initiated to address a need (personal or organizational): painting a room, organizing a party, planning a wedding, analyzing market demands to develop a new product, or recognizing an organizational need to train staff
- discussed the relationship between a cooking project and PM

What is Project Management?

Project management offers a competitive advantage in this fast-paced, quick-to-market environment; however, it is not a new concept. The idea of managing projects, which has been around for many centuries, was formalized and popularized by NASA and the US Department of Defense in the 1950s.

Before we dive in, let's examine some historical events that were crucial to the field's development.

Historical Perspective

Project management has undergone many evolutions prior to arriving at its current condition. Although there have been exceptional projects over the years—the Egyptian pyramids, Great Wall of China, Hoover Dam, and Pacific Railroad—project management was not recognized as a formal process until late twentieth century when organizations began to apply systematic project management tools and techniques to complex projects. As a discipline, organizations started to apply modern project management principles and tools to manage small and complex projects in different fields, including construction, engineering, and defense.

Define and Justify

In recent years, the world has become highly competitive as companies search for ways to convert potential opportunities into profitable products and services. Project management is built as a disciplined approach to managing activities, enabling organizations to transform great ideas into a new product or service or to improve a process.

> *Practitioners understand that an effective project management technique helps organizations carry out projects on time and on budget while also meeting business objectives. Increasingly, businesses of all sizes use the project management approach.*

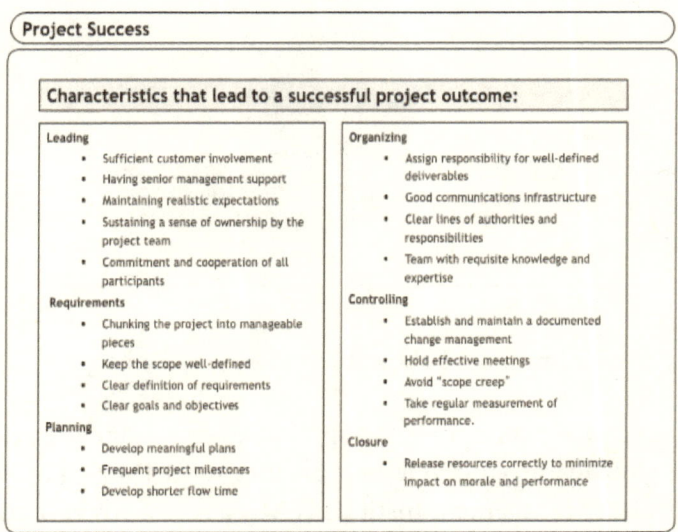

Project Success

Characteristics that lead to a successful project outcome:

Leading
- Sufficient customer involvement
- Having senior management support
- Maintaining realistic expectations
- Sustaining a sense of ownership by the project team
- Commitment and cooperation of all participants

Requirements
- Chunking the project into manageable pieces
- Keep the scope well-defined
- Clear definition of requirements
- Clear goals and objectives

Planning
- Develop meaningful plans
- Frequent project milestones
- Develop shorter flow time

Organizing
- Assign responsibility for well-defined deliverables
- Good communications infrastructure
- Clear lines of authorities and responsibilities
- Team with requisite knowledge and expertise

Controlling
- Establish and maintain a documented change management
- Hold effective meetings
- Avoid "scope creep"
- Take regular measurement of performance.

Closure
- Release resources correctly to minimize impact on morale and performance

Project management uses detailed, well-tested, systematic methodologies to drive ventures to successful completion. For example, a formal structure can advance the following project activities:

- facilitate a framework for the deliverables
- define the scope of work
- define ownership of various project activities
- ensure the final product delivers what the user requested

The opposing output could lead to project failure. (See figure below.)

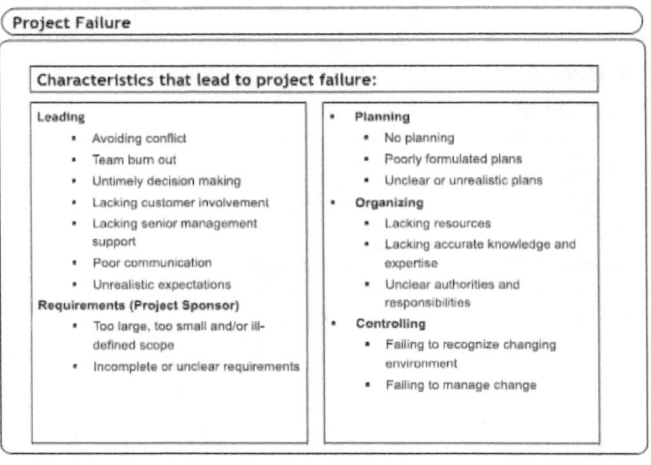

Elaboration on Project Management Concept

Managing projects requires the application of a standard process that is globally recognized as best practice for delivering projects. The Project Management Institute (PMI) is a globally recognized organization that offers credentials to project managers who have demonstrated the appropriate level of competency in both the real world and the academic world.

PMI defines project management as "the application of knowledge, skills, tools, and techniques to project activities to meet the project requirements" (*A Guide to the Project Management Body of Knowledge*, fifth edition).

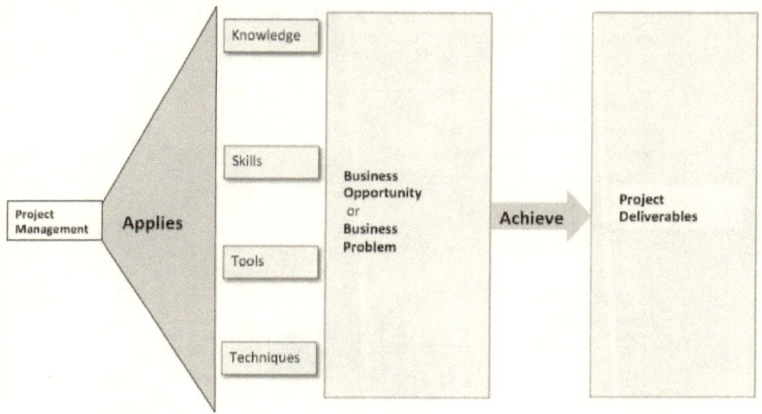

- *Tools* include templates such as Gantt Charts and MS Project schedule tools are used to facilitate activities.
- *Skills* describe the learned ability to carry out a task, the art and science of how you get things done.
- *Knowledge* encompasses facts and understanding acquired by a person through experience or education—the theoretical or practical understanding of a subject.
- *Techniques* include the process and methodology required to guide the project delivery skillfully in applying fundamentals to an activity.

Project management techniques aim to achieve predictable results by effectively coordinating resources. The artistry of communication that is required to lead people melds with the scientific techniques that provide a framework for the process. The human component adds a layer of complexity that guarantees projects can never be fully controlled. Ultimately, a project manager must rely on good judgment, interpersonal skills, and personal intuition to develop and execute a work plan.

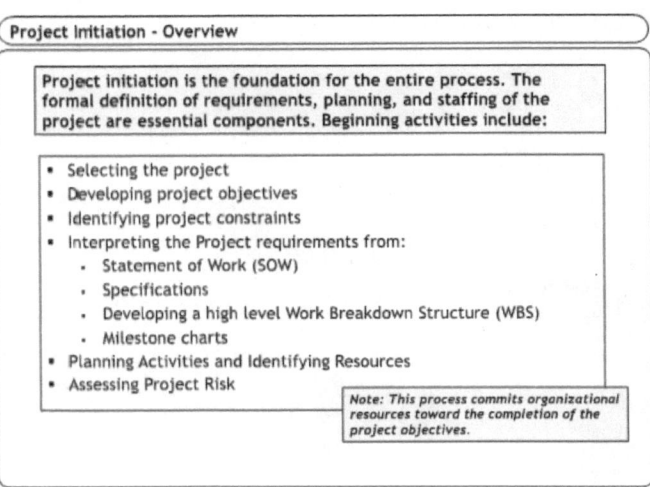

Project Initiation - Overview

Project initiation is the foundation for the entire process. The formal definition of requirements, planning, and staffing of the project are essential components. Beginning activities include:

- Selecting the project
- Developing project objectives
- Identifying project constraints
- Interpreting the Project requirements from:
  - Statement of Work (SOW)
  - Specifications
  - Developing a high level Work Breakdown Structure (WBS)
  - Milestone charts
- Planning Activities and Identifying Resources
- Assessing Project Risk

Note: This process commits organizational resources toward the completion of the project objectives.

While project management is a proven process designed to increase a positive project outcome, it is not a panacea for every situation an organization might encounter. (See box below.) The project management process begins with first defining the project and building the work plan. Project management is concerned with getting the project done in as effective a manner as possible— on time, within budget, according to specifications, and to the satisfaction of clients or stakeholders. However, there are situations in which the use of project management may not be appropriate.

> *Project management should not be used when people analyze the situation and develop a solution before thoroughly understanding the problem.*

Transitioning from Project Management to Project Management Framework is much different from managing other organizational activities. The goal of project management is to assemble a team that can deliver on the project goals and objectives, period! However, it should be noted that this goal has constrained factors, such as tight schedules or time pressures, delivering what was asked (scope) within the allocated budget, and providing results of acceptable quality.

> *Note: Product quality should not be compromised to meet deadlines and budgets. Poor product quality will render the project a failure.*

Project Requirement Formats

Project requirements can be provided in a variety of formats. It is the project manager's job to interpret these requirement.

This idea of managing projects is not new; in fact, you've done this at an early age and continue today. In these instances, our actions are often subject to subconscious improvisation that could lead to a wide array of results. Therefore, organizations implement framework that conduct structured deliveries of processes and yield highly probable outcomes in order to temper confusion. The focus obtained through structure has led to remarkable feats in a field that still lives in its infancy.

Key Lessons

- What is project management? It is simply a process! Project management encompasses managing day-to-day activities of the project to produce quality deliverables on time and within budget, and it's the responsibility of the project manager to ensure the project outcome is successful.
- Why use project management? Simply stated, it is the application of a proven, repeatable methodology to achieve project goals.
- The objective of project management is to optimize project success: quality requirements, approved budget, approved scope of work, and timely delivery.

Project Management Framework

This section provides a rudimentary definition of the project management framework, presented as "Knowledge Areas and Project Lifecycle" in the PMBOK.

Birth of a Project

Projects are initiated to produce a new product or service, improve a process, generate revenue, and/or save money. For businesses and organizations, projects are created to align with the mission and objectives of the company; the same applies to individual projects.

Projects should add value! One may choose to remodel a kitchen, prepare a healthy meal for twenty guests, or even paint a room; any project decision should align with the overall mission and objectives that you or the company try to achieve. Projects are the key to success for many organizations and must support the firm's mission and strategy of creating something new, controlling costs, improving processes, and generating revenue. Project initiation starts with a proposal or statement of work (SOW) that serves as a document used to capture project requirements.

Project Objectives

Project objectives are the criteria that must be met for the project to be considered successful. The project objective must be SMART (Specific, Measurable, Agreed upon, Realistic, and Time-limited)

- **Specific:** The objective must be clear enough for anyone with basic knowledge of the project can understand them.
- **Measurable:** The objective must be defined in measurable terms. To be successful, you must be able to measure and report on the progress.
- **Actionable:** There must be an agreement between the project manager, clients, and customers that the end result will will solve the problem or respond to the business opportunity.
- **Realistic:** The project objectives must be possible to achieve, with the available resources, knowledge, skills, and time.
- **Time-limited:** The objectives need to be framed with the clear time (cost) goals.

C&J brunch is no exception: the added value is nourishing the guests and recounting memorable experiences over good food shared with high school friends.

In many organizations, the birth of a project takes on a more formal process in the creation of a project charter—a document that formally recognizes a project, includes a problem statement, projects objectives, benefits, process owners, and a project sponsor or champion. C&J brunch is less formal and may not require a project charter, as this is the art part of project management where experience can override the science (formal step by step) aspect of project management.

In the process, C&J brunch will be used to introduce the initiation phase of a project in some details. Subsequent phases will be highlighted at a very high level, since these will be detailed in future handbooks.

Project management offers ancillary benefits beyond career progression. On a personal level, it helps to skirt the minutia of everyday life in order to obtain nourishment. This is often the objective of any endeavor. As varied as the conditions of a circumstance may seem, our purpose for embarking on any endeavor is to help someone or something progress toward a better condition.

Just think about the reason you attended school or have your current job (or are working toward the position that you desire). The incentive of a perceived improved condition often takes us from point A to point B.

Now bring this consideration to a microlevel. One could argue that you have already spent much of your life as a project manager. You have presided in spaces where the achievement of optimal objectives through the effective management of priorities and processes is crucial for your well-being.

Could you guess which of these spaces you've likely honed your PM skills the longest? Have you guessed it? Why, cooking, of course! From ordering food to preparing a large meal, the consumption of meals requires you to utilize innate and fundamental PM skills in order to achieve nourishment. Consider the process of eating.

- *Initiation:* Have an appetite.
- *Planning:* Search for a recipe or restaurant based on your appetite to replenish your hunger. Determine how to achieve your goal by considering the constraints and optimal quantity of required resources needed to satisfy your hunger.
- *Monitor and Control:* Constantly check on all other activities, and ask yourself some basic questions: Do you have all the ingredients? Is the cooking progressing well? Is anything missing? What adjustments do you need to make?

- *Execute and Act:* Make the food or travel to a restaurant where someone can prepare a meal for you.
- *Closeout:* My favorite part—when the meal is all done, it is time to chow down!

The term or duration of any venture is often segmented into five phases known as the project life cycle. This timeline facilitates the sequential arrangement of activities toward predetermined goals and deliverables.

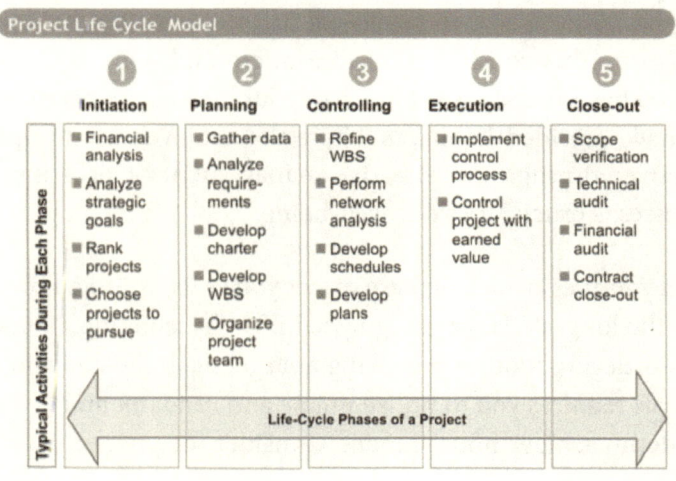

	Initiation	**Planning**	**Controlling**	**Execution**	**Close-out**
Typical Activities During Each Phase	■ Financial analysis ■ Analyze strategic goals ■ Rank projects ■ Choose projects to pursue	■ Gather data ■ Analyze require-ments ■ Develop charter ■ Develop WBS ■ Organize project team	■ Refine WBS ■ Perform network analysis ■ Develop schedules ■ Develop plans	■ Implement control process ■ Control project with earned value	■ Scope verification ■ Technical audit ■ Financial audit ■ Contract close-out

Life-Cycle Phases of a Project

The initiation is usually not included in the life cycle because many companies do not regard a project as such until after the initiation or decision has been made to pursue a project.

Four elements are defined during the initiation phase:

- need
- appropriate response
- major deliverables
- work groups

In the meal example, the menu outlines expectations and identifies stakeholders (those who will be impacted by the project). This document acts as C&J's project charter by verifying the output expectations.

- During the planning phase, the project solution is further developed based on stakeholder specifications.
    - o In the meal example, individual recipes are discovered in order to lay out a method of best achieving our ideal state. These recipes are packed with many of the materials included in a project plan.
    - o Scope and constraints are outlined based on serving size, dietary restrictions, and appliance availability.
    - o Cooking and baking times and cost of ingredients are also outlined to focus the inputs such that they result in an optimal output.
- During the controlling phase, the project plan is further refined to reflect the current condition of the project.
- Accrual of the list of ingredients serves as the final preexecution stage. This stage would include the list of ingredients, portion size, brand, and taste, as these details are tantamount to the project meeting its expectations.

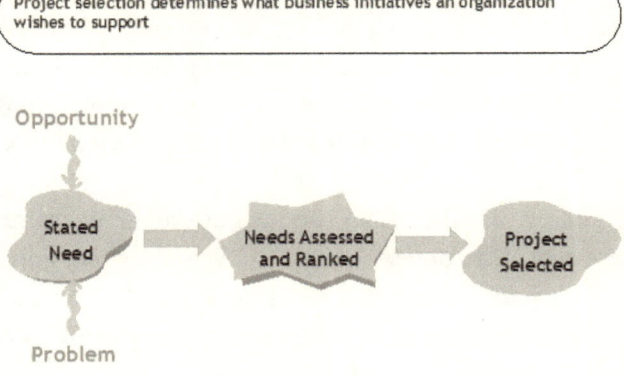

Project selection determines what business initiatives an organization wishes to support

Opportunity

Stated Need → Needs Assessed and Ranked → Project Selected

Problem

- During the execution phase, the defined work is performed.
  - o One final check of the ingredients, recipe, and menu will enable seamless delivery of the penultimate phase: execution. In this phase, C&J must be sure to follow all the instructions in cooking meals. The tasks that are described in the recipe must be clear—the less ambiguous the steps, the more likely the goal will be reached. A final check of the menu and images of the food will help to confirm expectations.

- During the closeout phase, emphasis is placed on verifying that the project will satisfy the required objective.
  - o Last but not least, you have to eat, right? C&J will be able to reevaluate the meal and preparation during and after the brunch through feedback and self-evaluation. This is a crucial (albeit oft-overlooked) phase, as it will provide key lessons and enable progress in subsequent similar endeavors.

PM delves much deeper than the five-stage life cycle. At a granular level, processes are associated with the ten knowledge areas of project management that the PMBOK guide defines as required expertise for project managers. Collectively, these knowledge areas can be regarded as a file cabinet containing forty-seven folders, with each knowledge area having multiple file folders in the drawer. These folders contain numerous processes—techniques, templates, and tools—that can be applied to a project. In the fifth edition of PMBOK, PMI defined the ten knowledge areas.

- The picture illustrates the idea of the file drawer concept mentioned above. The file drawer is visited, and needed information extracted to complete a desired output for the project. In this case, the creation of the project charter in the initiation phase requires information from scope, human resource, and procurement management.

Knowledge Areas

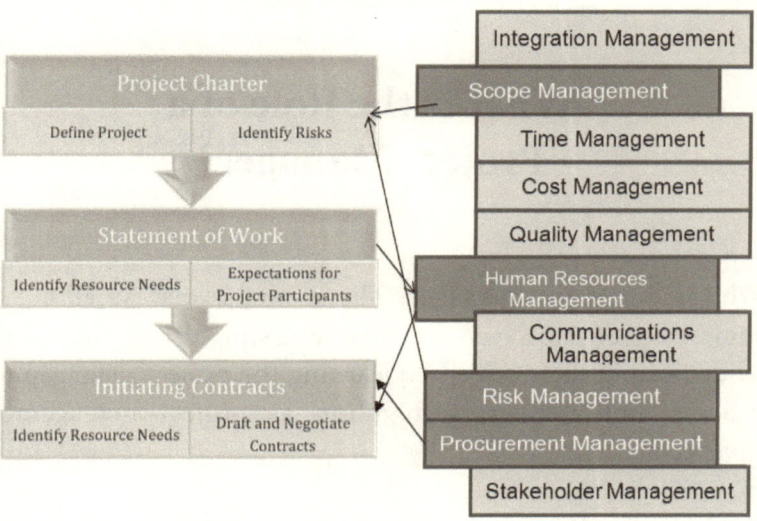

Note: While four knowledge areas are pulled out in this example, it does not mean that the rest are not needed. Each management area outlines the guidelines that are produced and/or applied to some degree during the course of any project. Good project management practice requires that the project manager review other knowledge areas to determine what might be appropriate for the project based on its size and complexity. This is the art of project management where experience helps to guide the level of tools needed for the project.

What is the Role of a Project Manager?

Who is the project manager? The answer is that we all are, in some respect. However, some have distinguished themselves by dedicating their careers to learning the project management process and attained recognition as project management professionals.

A project needs someone to be responsible for coordinating its activities, tracking progress, leading problem-solving and decision-making efforts, and accepting accountability for the overall results. That person is the project manager.

Project managers must plan, organize, evaluate, lead, direct, and control their projects, just as their counterparts in general management, functional managers. In similar fashion to the breakdown of project, program, and portfolio management, functional managers maintain oversight for project managers. General and functional managers are the bosses of any member or project-manager-led team. This person typically leads a specific work group, such as marketing, software development, or engineering, and he or she supports disciplines such as law, strategic planning, logistics, or human resource management.

Project Management Differs from General (Functional) Management

Project Manager:	**General/Functional Manager:**
Completes project activities by using knowledge and practices – such as, critical path analysis and Work Breakdown Structures (WBS) – that meet project requirements. They interface with managers/sponsor and must manage resources without authority of performance reviews.	Uses knowledge and practices to support the business through management of a specific function (such as accounting, manufacturing, marketing). Contrary to PM's, Functional Managers have direct reports with typical responsibilities such as performance reviews.

An accidental project manager is a person who is placed into the role of project manager by organizational necessity and chance rather than by design or through choice of career path. In some organizations, the functional manager will be viewed as the project manager simply because the roles may mirror each other, but as the table above shows, there are significant differences.

What are the roles and responsibilities of the project manager? In a nutshell, the project manager is responsible for the overall success or failure of the project! She or he is responsible for applying the project management process and principles of knowledge, skills, tools, and techniques during the course to maximize resource efficiencies and success of the project. The PM roles and responsibilities include (but are not limited to) the following:

1. Planning and developing all project deliverables.
2. Taking responsibility for the success or failure of the project, as this person is empowered to effectively perform project management activities.

Key Project Management Functions

Project Management is comprised of planning, organizing, monitoring, and controlling

Planning

planning

What do I have to do?

Controlling

Monitoring

Organizing

How can I get my arms around this work?

How do I stay on track to achieve my objectives?

How is the project progressing?

3. Budgeting, creating a work plan, and all project management procedures (scope management, issues management, risk management, etc.).
4. Taking responsibility for managing the project. He or she is the planner, organizer, monitor, and controller of project execution activities and resources to meet established costs, time frames, and quality goals.
5. Meeting the approved objectives of the project, including proper scope, budget, and schedule.

Now that we have established the various roles and responsibilities, let's discuss the characteristics of an effective project manager.

Successful Characteristics for a Project Manager

- Results oriented, can-do individual
- Strong commitment to project
- Ability to cope with ambiguity, setbacks and disappointments

- Planning
- Coordinating and organizing
- Client focused

- Supporting
- Coaching
- Delegating
- Directing

- Communicating
- Negotiating
- Commanding Respect
- Leading

- Calm when others are not
- Non-judgmental
- Creative thinker

(Diagram labels: Management, Leadership, Organizational, Personal, Interpersonal)

Characteristics of an effective project manager include the following:

- excellent communication skills (written and verbal)
- understanding of staff needs
- clear head for details
- strong commitment to the project
- ability to cope with ambiguity, setbacks, and disappointments
- awareness of organization goals
- can-do, results-oriented attitude
- cost consciousness
- political savvy and knowledge of how to influence others
- excellent negotiation skills
- ability to lead teams autonomously

Project Manager Communication Activities

> Project Managers must communicate throughout the project life-cycle. Principle communication activities include:

- Delivering project plans to team members and stakeholders
- Reissuing project plan components as necessary
- Receiving status on progress and cost
- Providing status to stakeholders, team members and executives
- Maintaining communication with team members and stakeholders
- Establishing clear communication channels
- Mitigating difficulties with technical language

- Oral and written communication is crucial for project managers.
- Project managers spend about 90 percent of their time acquiring and communicating information. This includes about two hours a day in meetings and more than one hour a day in one-on-one coaching or interviewing sessions.
- The project manager is the key to all project communications and must be skilled at effective communication with the following:
  - o senior management
  - o the project team
  - o competing project teams (peers)
  - o the customer
- Excellent communication skills are paramount to being an effective project manager. Here are key action steps to ensure effective communication:

Action Steps for Effective

- Prepare your message in advance
- Time your message carefully
- Deliver the message in a clear and constructive way (Be aware of the other persons, feelings, values and personality)
- Choose an appropriate mode of transmission
- Listen carefully for feedback from receiver
- Verify understanding by summarizing or paraphrasing, to make sure your message is understood

Effectiveness of communication methods

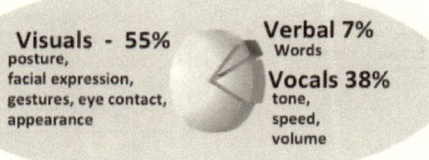

Visuals - 55%
posture,
facial expression,
gestures, eye contact,
appearance

Verbal 7%
Words

Vocals 38%
tone,
speed,
volume

- Individuals respond to different types of communication.
- In general, nonverbal actions speak louder than words.
- Preparing the message in advance will help ensure successful communication.
- Timing of message delivery is important and should be appropriate for the situation.
- Active listening skills are crucial, as audience responses will indicate whether the intended message is understood.
- At all levels, communication is key and is the top-line characteristic of successful project managers. The communications plan outlines how and when information will be shared with the project team.

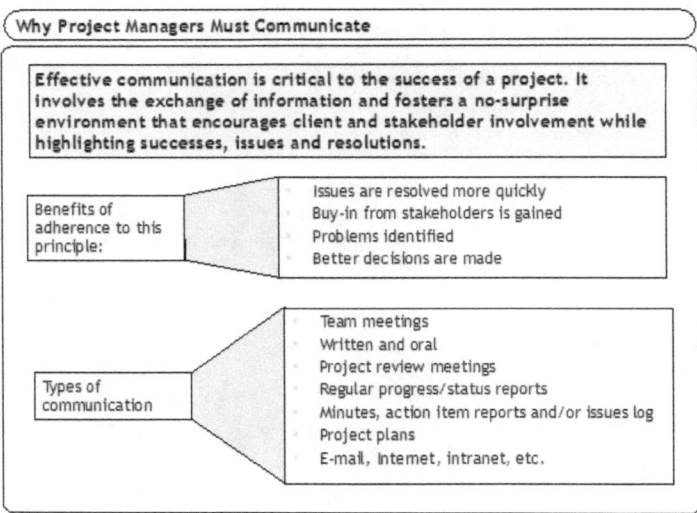

- The project manager must be proactive in communicating project information. Effective communication (regarding status, problems, successes, and dependencies) supports a low-risk environment through the involvement of all stakeholders and team members. Through these various avenues, communication confirms the needs and deadlines of project stakeholders by fostering an atmosphere that enhances team consensus.

One of the most important things a project manager can do is recognize that interfaces are a big part of project's life. The interfaces are more obvious in some scenarios than others. However, in all instances, they must be managed!

Stakeholders are the people who interface with the project manager. In some situations, a department of people can represent the stakeholders. For ease of understanding, the people represent the interfaces. Here is an illustration of various interfaces that a project manager could encounter on a project.

Managing Project Interfaces: Project interfaces are areas of interaction for the Project Manager. They possess potential for both success and failure.

An interface or interface group

- stands to gain or lose through the success or failure of the project,
- provides funding for the project,
- has invested resources in the project,
- participates in or works on the project,
- is affected by the outputs of the project,
- is affected by the outcome of the project, and
- is in the chain of accountability.

Chain of accountability: everyone who signs off to approve the project is viewed as being accountable for the project. This term relates to an interesting twist on the interpretation of "stakeholder" and its political implications. Several signatures must be secured before a project is finally considered approved.

> *Project managers face a variety of challenges, including having to negotiate their job in a political environment. Unlike functional managers, a project manager's job is temporary, just like the project. The job could disappear if the project is cancelled or is clearly failing.*

Key Lessons

- The project manager is the person with the responsibility and authority to deliver the project results.
- The project manager applies a project management process, uses appropriate methods to plan and execute the project, guides problem-solving decisions, and involves others as needed.
- Effective communication, both formal and casual, is essential to the success of a project.

Key Takeaways from This Book

What Is a Project?

A project has the following characteristics that differentiate it from a nonproject: a desired outcome or objective, limited duration (beginning and end), fixed budget, and allocated resources to perform the work.

What Is Project Management?

Project management is a systematic process that can be applied repeatedly to a project to deliver required goals. The aim is to achieve predictable results by effectively coordinating and applying resources.

Project Management Framework

The premise of the project management framework is based on the notion that projects go through a life cycle: initiation, planning, monitoring/controlling, execution/implementation, and closeout. Additionally, PMBOK provides ten knowledge areas that contain recommended techniques, templates, and tools that can be used to drive project activities.

Roles and Responsibilities of a Project Manager

Project managers are tasked with the responsibility of delivering the project objectives! They are responsible for properly applying the project management framework while employing the art and making reasonable decisions to ensure project success.

Implication for the Practitioner

Project management will continue to guide the way businesses operate by offering a premier solution in business operations. Frequent changes in technology, such as the need to get a product to market faster, have spurred the ubiquity of project management practice in various industries.

As globalization continues to bring people closer worldwide, the need and challenge for increased speed-to-market new product and service creation will only become more prevalent. Simultaneously, as global economic pressures push work offshore to low-cost countries, teams will become even more diverse and spread across the world, presenting an added layer of complexity that makes projects increasingly difficult to manage. Ultimately, change remains the only constant, and project management will need to keep pace with evolution.

The skills you have honed in nourishing yourself should afford you the necessary confidence to embark on the oft-applicable field of project management.

Preface to Other Books in Series

Each handbook will explore various critical project management functions required to ensure project success. In this handbook, the initiation phase was introduced to provide the reader with an insight on how a project is born. The image below provides a preview of the next series, which will focus on project plan development.

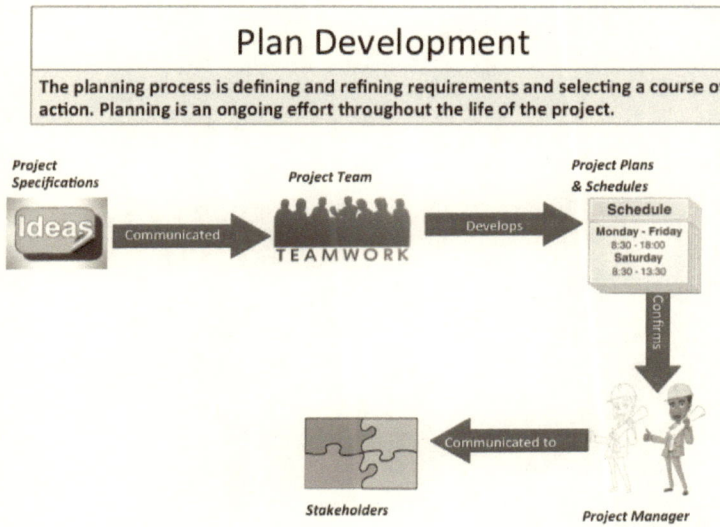

The further reading and references list provides complementary resources to support your understanding of project management, while additional books in this series will expand on this playbook of best practices.

Need to Learn More?

Do you need to dig deeper? Below are selected sources for further reading for a deeper exploration of a particular concept discussed in this series.

Sources

Fairley, R. E. 2009. *Managing and Leading Software Projects.* Hoboken, New Jersey: John Wiley and Sons, Inc.

Frame, J. D. 1995. *Managing Projects in Organizations: How to make the best of time, techniques, and people.* San Francisco: Jossey-Bass Publishers.

Kerzner, H., and F. P. Saladis. 2009. *Value-Driven Project Management,* 6th ed. Hoboken, New Jersey: John Wiley and Sons, Inc.

Kerzner, H. 1998. *Project Management: A Systems Approach to Planning, Scheduling, and Controlling,* 6th ed. Hoboken, New Jersey: John Wiley and Sons, Inc.

Meredith, Jack, and Samuel J. Mantel. 1995. *Project Management: A Managerial Approach,* 6th ed. Hoboken, New Jersey: John Wiley and Sons, Inc.

Project Management Institute. 2013. *A Guide to the Project Management Body of Knowledge,* 5th ed. Newtown Square, Pennsylvania: Project Management Institute.

Shtub, A., J. F. Bard, and S. Globerson. 2005. *Project Management: Process, Methods, and Economics.* Upper Saddle River, New Jersey: Person Prentice Hall.

Glossary of Terms

art: The application of personal experiences to the how.

budget or **cost:** Approved amount allocated to complete a project.

objective: The outcome toward which all efforts and resources are coordinated in an organization to reach its mission.

PMBOK guide: *A Guide to the Project Management Body of Knowledge*, published by the Project Management Institute, a book on the knowledge of project management.

PMI: The Project Management Institute, an international professional society for project managers.

PMP: Project Management Professional, a certification provided by PMI to those who demonstrate commitment to the profession and pass a comprehensive exam.

portfolio: A collection or group of projects and/or programs that meet a specific goal or objective and share common resources with common inputs.

practitioner: An actual user or anyone who consciously and repeatedly incorporates the prescribed process to manage projects.

PRINCE2: A body of knowledge that is used primarily in the United Kingdom. In contrast to PMBOK, PRINCE2 is a process-driven PM method that describes what the project manager and other major stakeholders should know and do in projects.

program: A collection or group of projects that contribute to higher interrelated goals with a common output that are managed using the same techniques in a coordinated fashion.

project charter: A document that formally recognizes a project; identifies the scope of the project; and includes a problem statement, project objectives, benefits, team members, process owners, and a project sponsor or champion.

project life cycle: A progression through a series of differing stages of development that continues through the life of the project, typically from initiation to closure.

project management: The act of collaborating among people and other required resources such that a project is planned, organized, and controlled effectively to accomplish project goals and objectives.

project value: The prize or benefit(s) derived from a completed project.

science: Application of the underlying prescribed principles of a project-management process to the why.

SOW: Statement of work, a description of the product or services to be delivered by the project.

About the Author

Chiji A. Ohayia, Ph.D., PMP, began his Project Management career as an Assistant Project Coordinator with the New York City Department of Sanitation and has more than 30 years of combined experience as a Project Management practitioner, consultant, and university professor. Dr. Ohayia has domestic and international experience in a range of sectors: health care, financial services, insurance, telecommunications, government agencies, and nonprofit organizations.

As an educator, he has been involved in course design and delivering project management, business, information technology, and organizational management courses to more than 25,000 students.

Dr. Ohayia serves as the President of SmartSolutions Enterprise, a consulting company specializing in project management, information technology, and diversity and inclusion management. He is also involved in a number of nonprofit organizations both in the United States and abroad.

Dr. Ohayia completed his PhD at Capella University and received his Master's and undergraduate degrees from Stony Brook University. He also holds a Master's Certificate in Project Management from George Washington University and has been a certified Project Management Professional since 2001.